AF439554

HAPPY TO BE ME

An Indigo Blue Adventure

Haven 101 Press ~ Rockville

BY
TOM DOYLE

ART BY
POLINA POVSHEDNA

To Alexis and Dominic,
forever my inspiration

My eyes open wide

as I wake for the day,

I know in my heart what I always say.

"How wonderful the day will be

and how happy I am

so happy to be me."

I look in the mirror,

my hair tossed this way and that.

Why would I ever cover it up with a hat?

A perfect mess, the way I like it best.

I am so happy, happy to be me.

What clothes should I wear?

My polka dot shirt with a bear?

One sock purple, one sock blue,

they don't have to match my shoe.

The clothes I pick out

make me want to shout!

What I wear that others see

aren't what make me, me.

I am so happy, happy to be me.

Maybe today I will run or skip to school,

even if others may look and say,

"She is not cool..."

It does not matter because

I smile and laugh,

and know whatever I hear,

whatever I see,

I am so happy, happy to be me.

LUNCH

Sometimes people may

whisper, point, and chuckle at me,

but I am not bothered

by what they see,

because I know

I am so happy, happy to be me.

SCHOOL

Some days I like to go climb a tree,

as if it's a ladder there just for me.

Other times I may jump, spin, and run.

All of these are so much fun!

As I do what I do and see what I see,

I think to myself how happy I am.

I am so happy, happy to be me.

I love how the world is for everyone,

no matter how near or far.

Every person and animal

are beautiful just as they are,

part of the same puzzle

all different colors and shapes,

fitting right into place.

I am so happy, happy to be me.

There are days I may get mad,

and feel a bit sad,

when it is hard to be happy and glad.

If I feel this way,

that is okay

because I always remember

how happy I am.

I am so happy, happy to be me.

Some nights before I go to bed,

I like to stand up on my head

because if I have a frown,

it will turn it around.

Then I can smile and think

how wonderfully wonderful life can be,

and how happy I am.

I am so happy, happy to be me.

Now that you know so much about me,

there is one more thing

for you to see.

Turn to the next page and

know this is true...

My name is Indigo Blue,

and just as I am happy,

happy to be me,

you should feel so happy,

happy to be YOU!

PUT YOUR
PHOTO HERE

Indigo Blue Adventures

Happy to Be Me

Happy Kindness Day

Indigo Blue and Demontreus Too!

Visit us!

Website: IndigoBlueAdventures.com

Instagram: @indigoblueadventures

Meet the Creators of *Indigo Blue Adventures*

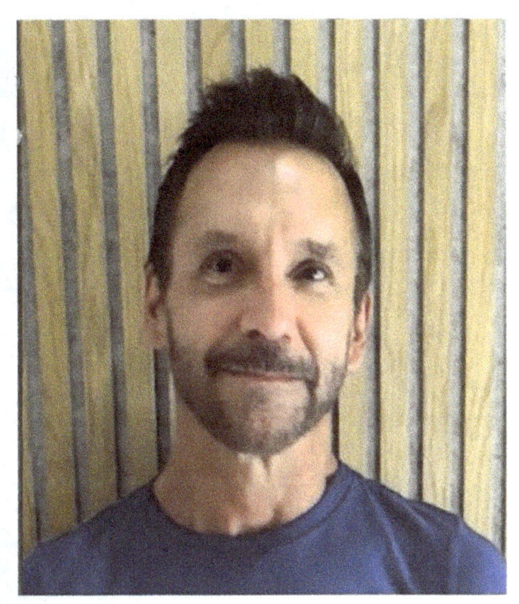

Tom Doyle, a native of the Washington DC area, is not only an accomplished trial lawyer but also a passionate author of children's books. Inspired by his experiences reading with his own children, he strives to empower young minds to embrace their uniqueness and become the best versions of themselves. Beyond his professional life, Tom finds fulfillment in his spiritual journey and serving the world around him. He is the creator of EquanimiChi, a breath to movement system, and also offers various other healing practices at Haven 101, the Wellness Center he founded.

Polina Povshedna is a children's illustrator from Odesa, Ukraine. She believes that youth literature serves as a great opportunity to stop, relax, and spend quality time with children, learn something with them and discuss their emotions. Polina and her own children read books before bed every evening and it is her favorite part of the day. She loves seeing the world through children's eyes and creating something for children that will evoke their emotions. Her dream is to write and illustrate her own book and dedicate it to her children.